Q&A: AN ESSENTIAL RESOURCE FOR SILVA MIND CONTROL METHOD STUDENTS

Updated Edition with
Newest Silva Technique
The MentalVideo

Q&A: AN ESSENTIAL RESOURCE FOR SILVA MIND CONTROL METHOD STUDENTS

by Staff Lecturers of Silva Mind Control International Inc.

Compiled by José Silva and Ed Bernd Jr.

The book that answers your Questions about the best ways to use the Silva Mind Control techniques

By Staff Lecturers of Silva Mind Control International Inc.

Compiled by Jose Silva and Ed Bernd Jr.

Published 2026 by Gildan Media LLC
aka G&D Media
www.GandDmedia.com

Originally published in 1983 by the Institute of Psychorientology, Inc. as Q&A: The book that answers your Questions about the best ways to use the Silva Mind Control techniques

New 2026 Edition with José Silva's Newest Technique: The MentalVideo

Front Cover design by David Rheinhardt of Pyrographx

Interior design by Meghan Day Healey of Story Horse, LLC.

Library of Congress Cataloging-in-Publication Data is available upon request

ISBN: 978-1-7225-0767-1

10 9 8 7 6 5 4 3 2 1

Contents

Introduction

This could be the most useful Silva book in your library.

- "I programmed but didn't get results. Why doesn't my programming work?"
- "I don't visualize, so how can I be successful with the Silva techniques?"
- "I've heard that the Silva Mind Control can be used to harm people. Is this true? And should it be used to program others, even if you think it is for their own good?"

These and countless other questions are asked of Silva Mind Control Method Lecturers throughout the world in classes and at graduate group meetings.

Can I use the Silva techniques to:

- Find oil?
- Win a contest?
- Find my ideal mate?
- Find lost objects?

How do I program to:

- Improve my health
- Cure sleep walking, epilepsy, stuttering
- Help an intellectually disabled person

These and other questions are answered in this book.

These are some of the many questions that have been asked and answered through the years in the *Silva Mind Control Newsletter* and in more recent years the Silva Method UltraMind websites.

About the Contributors

José Silva, creator of the Silva Method of Self Mind Control and the Silva UltraMind ESP Systems, personally trained more than a hundred thousand people to develop and use more of their human potential.

He began his research in 1944, working first with his own ten children.

Then, for more than a decade, he trained people on an individual basis, researching and perfecting his method.

After that, he trained groups of twenty, still researching to make his method better and better.

In 1966 Silva began to travel extensively to share his findings with the world.

Three years later he began showing other people how to present the Silva training, and today his courses are taught in more than 100 countries around the world, and millions of people have benefited.

Certainly, there is no one in the world who knows more about the science of psychorientology than José Silva, the man who created this science. Look through these pages and read José Silva's answers to the questions you have about making better use of the Silva techniques.

Juan Silva is director of foreign operations for the Silva organization, and has vast experience in helping Silva graduates learn more about Silva techniques.

He has been actively involved with Silva Mind Control since 1949, when his brother José used one of the techniques he was researching to help Juan overcome a serious health problem.

Juan then made a commitment that he would personally help at least one person a week with his knowledge of the techniques.

He still continues to fulfill his personal commitment to help individuals, as well as traveling the world to work with Silva graduates, instructors, and national directors to help bring these techniques to all the people on the planet.

You will benefit greatly when you study and apply the suggestions Juan Silva has for improving your life with the Silva techniques.

Ed Bernd Jr. is an author, journalist, lecturer, and editor of the *Mind Control Newsletter*. For several years he published the popular newsletter *Projections*, distributed by Silva Lecturers in many areas of the United States, and as far away as Guam.

An award-winning journalist, Bernd uses his skills to discern the important facts and present them clearly and in a way that they can be put to practical use.

He has been presenting Silva lectures since 1976, joined the world headquarters staff in 1981, and has been coordinator of the Silva International Graduate Association since 1982.

He also coauthored several books with both José Silva and José Silva Jr.

Harry McKnight was the first lecturer to join José Silva on the staff of Silva Mind Control, to present the Silva courses throughout the world. He has presented both the basic and advanced lectures worldwide.

With a background in theology and psychology, McKnight brings special insight to questions concerned with using the Silva techniques for development of our inner resources and strengths.

McKnight uses his talent for communication to help graduates gain greater understanding and insight in the use of the Silva techniques.

Chapter 1

Why Does Programming Sometimes Fail To Work?

by José Silva

Programming works. But we may not always work it properly. The first step in trouble-shooting your programming is to check your desire, belief, and expectancy.

Do you really desire what it is you are programming for, or are you just trying it for the fun of it? Is it important to you? Does it serve a purpose? Does it solve a problem?

Do you have a strong belief factor? Do you believe you are worthy of what you are seeking, or that the case merits a solution? Do you have any doubts regarding the case? Is your request fair? Is it best for all concerned?

All the ingredients must be right; then you will get your solution. You will get results as long as you are solving problems and helping the Creator in making this planet a better place to live.

Do you really expect it? That is sometimes a difficult factor to accept. You must program in the future in a past-tense sense. That is, you must "Try believing you have already received." You must have the Take it for granted" feeling. That does not mean to program hoping you will get it; it means to program knowing and feeling you have already gotten it.

You can program with either the Mirror of the Mind or the 3-Scenes Technique. I will illustrate with the Mirror of the Mind.

To keep your expectancy factor high, program in this manner:

First visualize (which means to recall what something looks like) the problem, or the existing situation that you need to improve, in the first scene—the blue-framed mirror.

Then erase that image, move the mirror to the left, change the frame to white, and create (with your imagination) and project onto the white-framed mirror your desired end result, or solution.

In the future, whenever you think of the project, at level or at any other time, then visualize the solution image you have created in the white-framed mirror.

Remember that you have already created and received your solution at your clairvoyant dimension; now just visualize it (recall what your solution looks like) in the white-framed mirror.

It is like ordering something from a catalog. You have ordered it, you know it is on the way, and it will show up in your physical environment soon.

The success of your programming is a result of all of the factors involved. The right ingredients, lightly programmed, will bring successful results. The wrong ingredients, strongly programmed, will not bring successful results.

When people have a very strong desire, because of a very strong need (such as the need to correct a life-threatening illness, for instance) then it does not require as strong an expectancy to obtain successful results. There is enough energy in the desire portion of the formula to insure success.

But when there is not such a strong desire, then it will take a greater expectancy to get results. For instance, if a person programs to win a contest when they do not really need to win the contest, then the belief and expectancy factors need to be stronger for the programming to be effective.

If a person programs for a $100,000-a-year job, but does not need the money and only wants to put it in the bank, then it will be difficult to achieve successful results. It would be better to work up to the ultimate goal in smaller steps, each step programmed according to your needs.

A careful study of the formula will reveal to you why some people get spectacular results with their programming when they first learn the technique, but then seem to be less successful later.

At first, they program for things they have a very strong need for, thus a very strong desire. This compensates for a modest expectancy factor.

If the initial success causes the person to develop very strong belief and expectancy factors, then future programming will also be successful.

As the problems become less important, it is more important that you include the right ingredients, applied properly, to your programming. It is more important then that you put more of your positive, expectant, energy into your programming.

As long as one of the three factors (desire, belief, expectancy) is very strong, it will carry the other two along with it. But all three must be present. This is a "tri-cycle" formula. Practice, and you will succeed.

How Often to Reinforce Your Programming

You can reinforce your programming in the following manner:

Whenever you happen to think of your project during the day, visualize your solution image framed in white.

You should go to level to reinforce your programming at least once every seventy-two hours. On important projects, it would be good to reinforce at level every night.

When doing this, be sure to imagine or recall the feeling you would associate with success; have a feeling that you have already received it.

At the beta dimension, you should have a positive expectancy; at the alpha dimension, you should have the attitude that the project has already been successfully completed.

You have planted a seed. At the subjective dimension, your project has been completed, now, physics is like soil and it will take time for the seed to grow through that "soil" and surface where it can be seen in the physical dimension.

Expect your results at beta, *accept* your results at alpha.

If, after a period of time, you have not seen any results, then add: "May the best thing happen for all concerned." Adopt the attitude that it has not worked so far, but from this day on the programming will succeed. You are adding another ingredient; you do not need to continue reinforcing your programming. The final result might be a modified result, because your original request was not best for all concerned.

Chapter 2

I Don't Visualize Well.
Is It Important To Visualize Well?
What Can I Do To Improve My Visualization?

by José Silva

Visualization seems to be the most powerful way to obtain the results you want from your programming.

Actually, there is no big mystery to visualization:

Visualization is simply remembering something you have seen before.

If you have seen it before and can remember what it looks like, then you are visualizing.

Visualizing with your mind is not the same as seeing with your eyes. You do not get the same kind of pictures.

Imagination Is Not The Same As Visualization

If you have to construct and image of what you think something might look like, that's imagination.

After you have done that, you can visualize your creation, by remembering what it looks like

That is exactly what we do with the Mirror of the Mind and the 3-Scenes techniques.

First you *visualize* the problem, by *recalling* what it looks like.

Then you use your *imagination* to *create* an image of the solution.

After that, all you do is *visualize* (recall) the solution image you created.

You can improve both visualization and imagination by practicing memory pegs. Recall what a glass of tea looks like. Then imagine the object you want to remember associated with it. That's visualization and imagination.

Chapter 3

How Can I Increase My Desire To Do Something?

by Juan Silva

This is something I had to do during some research José and I did many years ago to determine whether José could use Mind Control to make an inventor out of me. I had little desire to invent anything, so I had to find reasons to become an inventor, and increase my desire that way.

Let me give an example of how you might program to increase your desire for something. Let's say you want to get a new car. Perhaps you have three reasons for buying a new car, but that is not enough to stimulate a strong desire in you.

Then meditate on it, and at your level, come up with two or three more reasons for buying a car. Then you will have more desire.

For instance, perhaps you want a new car because you feel a new one will be more reliable and not leave you stranded so often. A new car might also be more comfortable, and might get better gas mileage.

Now enter your level and think about reasons to get a new car. Besides being more reliable, a new car might be much safer, not only because it will be less likely to break down and cause a wreck, but because it will be less likely to break down and leave you stranded in a dangerous area late at night. With those added reasons for getting a new car, you now have more desire.

In addition, you might realize that your old car is bad for your image as far as the people you do business with, your customers, or your employer. Thus an improved self image might be another reason to get a new car. This again increases your desire.

You might also decide that now you need another type of car than what you have, perhaps replacing your sedan with a station wagon. Again, this builds desire.

An increase in desire produces an increase in the energies you are directing towards your project, and gets you closer to your goals.

This is an approach you can apply to all areas of your life. For instance, after I developed enough desire to invent something, I sold my invention, a merchandising machine, to a firm in Mexico City. Then they hired me to run the factory to make the machines.

I used my Silva techniques in that position. I found it important to keep my desire high so that I could do a good job. Many times, I could have just given orders to resolve some difficulty, but I believe it is much better to encourage people to work out their own solutions through cooperation.

Sometimes I would go to my level and remind myself of the importance of taking this "cooperation" approach:

You may have a solution to a problem, but by cooperating with others, having dialogue and discussions with them, you may find that someone else has a better solution than you have, or an idea to make your solution more effective. This would increase my desire to spend more time and not be too impatient.

Some people find it easier than others to keep their desire high. But all of us can benefit from spending some time at level, taking things one step at a time as we program our desire, belief and expectancy so that our programming for our goals will be more powerful and more effective.

Chapter 4

How Can I Use The Silva Techniques To Help Me Find An Ideal Mate?

by José Silva

We know that for each person, there is a perfect partner somewhere, and each is looking for the other. We need to make it easy for the two to find each other. The best way we can think of to use the MentalVideo technique.

To use it, proceed in the following manner:

At beta, with your eyes open, mentally create, with visualization, a MentalVideo of a problem, or the existing situation. Include everything that belongs to the animate matter kingdom. Animate matter means everything that contains life.

After you have completed the MentalVideo of the problem, use visualization to review it at beta, with your eyes closed.

Later, when you are in bed and ready to go to sleep, go to your center with the 3 to 1 method. Once you are at your center, review the MentalVideo that you created of the problem, or the existing situation, when you were at the beta level. You can learn to use the 3 to 1 method and more at the SilvaNow.com website.

After you have reviewed the problem, mentally convert the problem into a project. Then create, with imagination, a MentalVideo of the solution.

The MentalVideo of the solution should contain a step-by-step procedure of how you desire the project to be resolved.

After both of the MentalVideos have been completed, go to sleep with the intention of delivering the MentalVideos to your tutor while you sleep. Take for granted that the delivery will be made.

During the next three days, look for indications that point to the solution. Every time you think of the project, think of the solution that you created in the MentalVideo, in a past tense sense.

Tips For Success

There is no need to specify the other person's characteristics. Many people have programmed that way, and found a person with the characteristics that were sought, only to find out that they had been asking for the wrong thing, once the person arrived.

If you send the information to High Intelligence about yourself, and when and where you will be available to meet your perfect partner, and allow sufficient time, then High Intelligence will know how to get this person to come in contact with you.

You are looking for your complementary partner, and that person is looking for you, but doesn't know how to contact you. You need to make it easier for this person.

Note: You can learn more about the Mental Video technique in our new book *Creative Coincidences*. For more information please see Resources (page 105).

Chapter 5

Why Do Silva Graduates, And Even Lecturers, Get Sick?

by Juan Silva

If a person could suddenly do everything after learning the Silva Mind Control Method techniques, then that would pretty much do away with our purpose for being here on earth, wouldn't it? That would remove the purpose of having God here, too, wouldn't it?

We are here to learn to use all of our abilities, and to learn by gaining a lot of experiences. Each of us comes with certain biological programming, and throughout life we acquire many experiences that influence our thoughts and actions. Therefore, each person has specific lessons in life.

Very often, the people who are adventurous and inventive will find that those traits can either get them into trouble, or can help them achieve great things. It depends on where the energy is directed. Such a people might, in fact, drop their guard by not programming in advance, especially before sleeping when they are more vulnerable, and might fail to get sufficient rest and ultimately let a cold virus slip past a weakened immune mechanism. Such a person might find their enthusiasm sometimes gets them into trouble in their relationship with others.

But the mark of a successful Mind Control practitioner is that they quickly recognize the situation and use the Silva techniques to bring things back into balance again. A person's life is not judged by how many times they stumble, but how many times they get up.

A person's life is measured by how much that person is doing to serve humanity. Notice that throughout history, the greatest people are not those who got a lot for themselves, but those who gave a lot of service to humanity.

This is not meant to excuse those who do not properly apply their Silva techniques to keep themselves healthy and productive. Those who put unnecessary stresses on their bodies, like smoking for instance, and claim that they use the Silva techniques to keep it from harming them, may just be fooling themselves. If they had that much control, they would be able to obtain whatever benefits they need without having to engage in a harmful, destructive habit.

But recognize that there are people who choose to live highly-stressful lifestyles in their efforts to serve humanity, and sometimes these people push themselves beyond the ability of their bodies to cope, and it is then that they get a message that they need to correct their ways.

Chapter 6

How Can I Use The Silva Techniques To Help A Person With Intellectual Disabilities?

by Ed Bernd Jr.

Keep in mind that a human being is more than a body and a brain. A human being also has soul, which we refer to as human intelligence. And this human intelligence has a mind. The mind is not biological; the mind is a faculty of human intelligence.

Biological intelligence is cell intelligence. It has stored knowledge of your life's experiences, including what you experience with your imagination. Human intelligence has its own recorded experiences. Biological intelligence functions in the physical (objective) dimension; human intelligence functions in the mental (subjective) dimension.

If the body or brain is damaged, this does not necessarily mean any blockage in the subjective dimension, where human intelligence resides. Damage to the brain may impede objective communications, but that does not necessarily mean it affects the mind.

We cannot draw a definite conclusion at this time as to whether the soul's growth is inhibited by a malfunction of the body or brain of a person. The person is still having experiences, though the experiences are perceived differently than they would be if the damage were not there. It could be that this person is getting the exact experiences they need to insure the appropriate growth of the soul into higher consciousness.

In using the Silva techniques to work with such a person, first go to your level and work on yourself so you will relate better to the other person, and will be better able to deal with that person. Communicate with the other person at level, in the subjective dimension, as you learn in the Silva ESP training.

Use your imagination to communicate with them. Use your other Silva techniques too: You can use the 3-Fingers Technique, for instance, when interacting with the other person. You can use Dream Control and the MentalVideo Techniques to obtain ideas to help the person.

You can also trigger dreams in the other person so that the person can be helped to be more self-guiding and self-sufficient.

And remember to maintain positive thoughts and a positive expectancy towards that person at all times; although some of the brain circuits might not be functioning properly, in the subjective dimension, at the soul level, that person is a genius.

Chapter 7

Why Are Some Subjects More Difficult To Detect In Case Working Than Other Subjects?

by José Silva

First, the operator might not have enough experience. The clairvoyant might not have enough experience in general to be as confident as necessary every time; or the clairvoyant might not be experienced in that particular kind of problem case. We need to establish points of reference for all of the various types of abnormalities to be sure of getting correct answers most of the time.

Second, consider how great the need is to solve the problem. Usually, it is easier to detect very serious problems than those that are less serious. When there is a serious problem, it is like the subject with the problem is crying out at the subjective level, seeking help. Those are the easiest to detect.

Third is the factor of compatibility, or rapport. The more you practice your case working, the more you become in empathy with different kinds of people/different kinds of auras. The more you practice—the more experience you have—the more you are able to function harmoniously with any subject.

Fourth, the clairvoyant might have a negative attitude towards certain types of problems. Sometimes these attitudes have existed since infancy. Again, practicing at level three times a day, and practicing case working as often as possible, will help overcome this.

Chapter 8

Is It Possible To Hurt Someone In The Subjective Dimension?

by José Silva

This question is often asked. No, you cannot hurt someone with your mind in the subjective dimension. It is impossible.

In the physical dimension, we need to push things into place. In the subjective dimension, it is just the opposite: in the subjective dimension, we use an attracting force.

When we push things, we can bend them. Or break them.

Everything that attracts works with natural laws. You can attract something to conform to a picture of perfection. You can attract something to conform to the pattern of the Soul Mold.

If you want to change something away from the original blueprint, you must push. And you must push from the physical dimension.

There are plenty of negative energy generators in the world. They push people around and hurt them with their bodies, with their words, with their facial expressions, even with the physical part of their aura. There are plenty of ways to hurt people. There are plenty of ways to cause problems. But these are in the physical dimension.

You can give people negative suggestions in the subjective dimension, but you cannot force them to accept those suggestions. If the person chooses to accept a negative suggestion, then that is their problem, not yours.

You can be assured that whenever you send a picture of perfect health, or what you believe is perfect health, in the subjective dimension, it can only help. If your picture doesn't fit the mold (the soul mold), it simply will not be accepted. Yet the energy you send can still have a positive effect.

Chapter 9

How Can I Use The Silva Techniques To Win Money And Other Prizes?

by José Silva

There are many ways to go about it. And there are many ways to qualify for it.

I have heard people say that if they won some money, they would give half of it to charity. The question is, what has that person done with the smaller amounts he or she has had so far? Does this person have a track record of doing just that?

There are many ways to qualify for it.

If you feel that your past actions (not your intentions, but your actions) qualify you to be worthy of winning money, then program for it.

You can use Dream Control Step 3, to obtain information about what contest you should enter, or what horse you should bet on.

Then you can program the desired end results in the Mirror of the Mind or the 3-Scenes Technique.

If you are betting on something like a football game or a horse race, you can work cases on the participants to give you information you can use.

Just remember, we are here to help solve problems on this planet. If you feel you need a million dollars, it is easy to get it: just give ten million dollars worth of service to humanity, and you'll get the money you need.

Chapter 10

Is It Moral To Program Other People, Or Is It Improper To Interfere With Their "Free Will"?

by Harry McKnight

We are here to solve problems on this planet. The only things that are immoral are creating problems, or failing to attempt to solve problems.

We know we are solving problems when we do things that are creative and constructive.

We are creating problems when we do things that are destructive.

As long as we are working to help correct things, to help relieve suffering, to make things right, we are doing what is "moral."

A person might feel they have a "right" to be ill, to suffer for some reason. We believe this is a mistaken attitude, and we should program to help them understand this error in their thinking.

When there are differences of opinion, and you are not sure who is correct, then look to the intention in your heart and program for what you believe is best. Consider that there may be a wider plan that you are unaware of. You might want to add a phrase such as, "If this is best for all concerned," or "May good come to all involved."

Note: If you have learned the MentalVideo Technique you can use it to turn the question over to Higher Intelligence for an answer. You can learn all about the MentalVideo in our newest book, *Creative Coincidences.* There is information about it in the Resources (page 105).

Chapter 11

How Can I Use The Silva Techniques To Find Lost Objects?

by Ed Bernd Jr.

There are a variety of techniques you can use. In an emergency, apply every technique you can think of.

You can enter your level and use your mental screen to recall the last time you remember having the object, and recall where you went from there.

You can use the 3-Fingers Technique, keeping the lost object in mind as you walk around looking for it. Also, you can program for success in locating it with the Mirror of the Mind or the 3-Scenes Technique.

You might want to program a dream to find it, provided you have practiced remembering dreams so you can use Dream Control Step 3 successfully.

Note: You can learn many of these techniques in the *Silva Choose Success Master Course.* There is information about it in the Resources (page 105).

You can also ask for help from another graduate. That happened here in the office.

Our switchboard operator, Christina, could not find her car keys and had to take a taxi to work. She said that she could usually locate lost objects by simply using her mental screen, but this time she did not get results that way.

Lucien Lamoureux, lecturer from Atlanta, GA, who was in Laredo for the International Convention, offered to help. Lucien went to his level, projected to where the keys were, and then drew a picture of what he visualized: a hanging lamp, and a bent tin pipe, like a stove pipe.

Chris looked amazed. "That lamp is in my living room!" she exclaimed. She called her husband, who was doubtful but checked anyway. Near the lamp was a bent tin can, on the floor . . . and the keys were inside.

Here is the drawing that Lucien made.

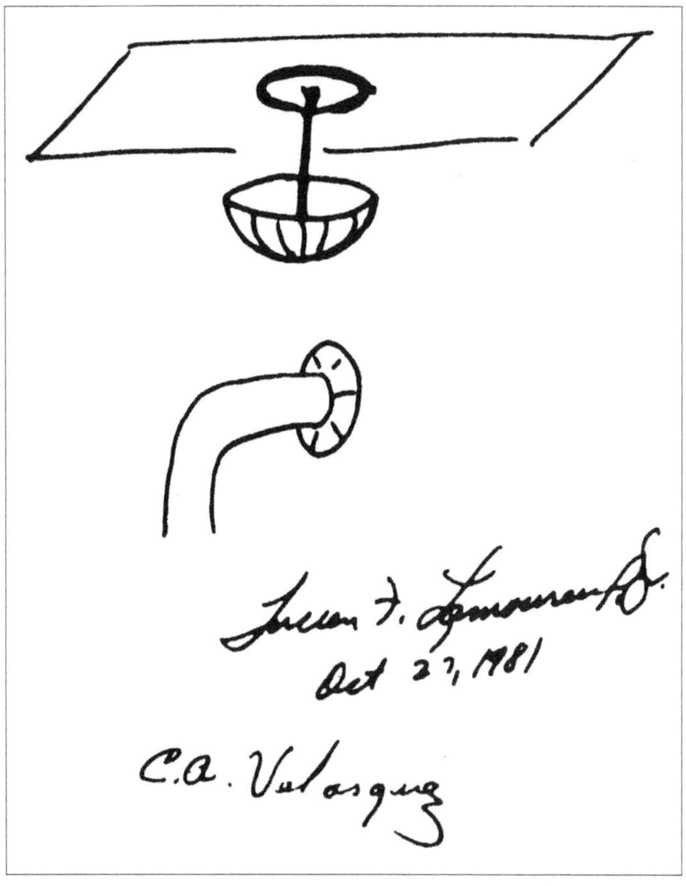
Oct 27, 1981

Chapter 12

Can The Silva Techniques Help Me Find Oil?

by José Silva

We have to establish points of reference first, so our first step is to train people to give the history of oil wells, without any prior knowledge of the wells. Psychics should learn to determine how long a well has been in operation, how much it produces, how deep it is, and the quality of the oil.

After that, psychics can begin to investigate the question of where to drill wells. This can be done by setting up a grid pattern on a map, then have psychics visualize different areas of the map to determine the best locations to drill.

It would be necessary for psychics to actually "explore" the area physically to find oil. Then determine the depth and other factors to see if it is feasible to drill for it.

It would be best to use a team of specially trained psychics, so their data could be correlated. This would help eliminate the error factor that is still found in this kind of work.

To be able to function as a psychic to detect oil, you should first make the objective and subjective investigations of oil as you did with metals and leaves in the ESP training. That is, get some crude oil, look at it, touch it, smell it. Then go to your level, review the objective impressions, then make subjective tests for light, temperature, odor and solidity of material.

We would like to train a group of psychics for this purpose. If there are people in the oil business who believe in what we are doing who would like to receive special training for oil exploration, contact us and we will make arrangements for training. We want to be able to monitor results and report on them.

Chapter 13

Can I Use Silva To Stop Stuttering?

by José Silva

Many graduates report they have stopped stuttering. We have had a lot of reports of success with this. Here is what you do:

Enter your level and program at your level that you will be able to practice reciting poems, or singing. You will practice the poetry or the singing at beta.

Memorize the poems or the songs, and practice.

The problem with stuttering, also known as stammering, is that people try to speak faster than they can handle it, and get stuck. They think faster than they can speak.

Those who stutter or stammer are afraid of stuttering or stammering, and being afraid triggers the situation and makes it worse.

Once the person has memorized the poem or song and knows exactly what they are going to say, they won't be afraid. The fear is gone. And if you program it at level, you will follow the program. It is important to memorize and recite it from memory, not read it.

Once you memorize what to say, you can pace yourself so you can recite it without stuttering or stammering. From there, you get the idea of how fast to talk. Confidence builds, and the problem is eliminated.

This probably will not work if you simply do it all at beta. It is important to program at the alpha level to deal with the problem. If the problem is caused by organic disorders, then other steps may be necessary to correct it.

Parents can help their children overcome these problems through several techniques.

The child's mother can program herself to awaken automatically during the night when the child is most receptive, then reenter her level and mentally project to the child to help.

You can also program a glass of water to be used as a reinforcing mechanism.

- At level, hold the glass of water as you learn in the advanced course.

- Visualize the child with the problem in a scene directly in front of you.
- Then in a scene to your left, visualize the child practicing to overcome the problem.
- In a final scene further to your left, imagine the child normal, with no more worry about the problem.

Chapter 14

Is There A Technique To Use To Stop A Person From Sleepwalking?

by José Silva

There are several techniques you can apply to this problem. Nobody knows what causes sleepwalking, but graduates have reported success correcting it with Silva techniques.

If you have a child who sleepwalks, help your child enter their level and then program them.

You can also program yourself just before going to sleep that you will awaken automatically when the child is most receptive and program them.

To program a child, tell them, at their level or while asleep and most receptive, what is happening, and that they will not do it any more.

Tell them that whenever they are about to start sleepwalking, they will awaken before it takes place. Tell them that as soon as it is about to happen, at the first indication, they will awaken.

You can also program a glass of water for this problem.

- At level, hold the glass of water as you learn in the advanced course.
- In the first scene, directly in front of you, visualize the child with the problem.
- In the second scene, to the left of the first, (to your, the operator's, left) visualize the child awakening before getting up.
- In the third scene, still further to your left, imagine the child normal with no more worry about the problem.

Then have the child drink the water before going to bed.

Chapter 15

I Have Recently Developed An Ulcer. What Is The Best Way To Work On It Using The Silva Techniques?

by José Silva

Usually, we find that when Silva Graduates have health problems, it is because they have not been practicing every day.

We recommend that everyone spend five, ten, or fifteen minutes a day at level. Five minutes is good; ten minutes is very good; fifteen minutes is excellent.

During that time, you should relax, maintain minimum mental activity, and be sure to stay at your level. You can use a recording of the "Alpha Sound" to help you stay at your level.

It is a good idea for all graduates to listen to the Long Relaxation Exercise (Silva Centering Exercise) once a week.

While at your level, you can practice relaxing by counting from 100 to 1.

Alpha Sound For Health

When working on any health problem, you can use the alpha sound recording.

Place the audio player directly over the affected area, at full volume. The electromagnetic pulsations coming from the speaker excites the sub-atomic particles. While doing this, visualize yourself in perfect health, and the problem area will fit into that mold you create and visualize.

Also practice working health cases during this time (as you learned in class). The more you visualize perfect health, the more your brain will work to create it for you.

Chapter 16

In Class, Why Do We Name All Those Diseases? Doesn't This Give Us Mental Pictures Of The Diseases?

by José Silva

We must cancel specific diseases. We cannot cancel them generally. You already have an idea of these diseases in your bio-computer, we must name specific ones so we can cancel them out.

If you had never heard of any of these diseases, you would not have to cancel them specifically.

Even if you have one of the diseases we mention, we still want to use the statements the way they are written. These statements build tools for us to use later to fight these diseases.

First, we need tools to use in this dimension, the subjective dimension. Then we can fight the disease.

If you have a disease that is not mentioned in the health statements, then add it in. Repeat it during a number of different practice sessions during the course, when you are at your Alpha level of mind. You need this tool.

These statements are not included in your Basic Lecture Series course manual, because once you have completed the Basic Lecture Series, you have created the tools you need. There is no need to use these statements any more.

If you like, each time you go to level, you can simply repeat this positive statement,

"I will always maintain a perfectly healthy body and mind."

Chapter 17

Can I Correct Health Problems With Symbolic Imagery?

by José Silva

Yes, you can do this. I know of many people who have successfully done this.

It is even better if you know anatomy well enough that you can visualize what is actually happening in your body.

If the patient doesn't know anatomy that well, the best thing is to have a doctor, or someone who does know anatomy well, to make a transfer to a symbolic image. This must be done at the subjective dimension. Both doctor and patient should go to level, and the doctor visualizes the actual physiology while explaining to the patient what images to use.

For instance, you can convert white blood cells to white mice, and a tumor to cheese. Then mentally picture the white mice eating up all the cheese.

This will work, but to have maximum effectiveness, the doctor should make the connection for the patient at level.

Chapter 18

Can Silva Techniques help Me Change My Personality?

by Ed Bernd Jr.

You bet! That is exactly what happened with me. And fortunately I've been able to verify the changes with psychometric testing.

About three years ago, I applied for a job as a newspaper advertising salesman so I could develop some sales skills and persuade more people to sign up for the Silva course, which I was presenting full time.

The advertising director of the newspaper had me take a personality test, one that took three hours to complete! When he read the results to me over the phone a few days later, I learned a lot about myself.

There were a lot of good things: "Really intelligent; very, very bright." There were other good things like loving and very energetic and a good communicator (probably talks too much, they added).

And then came a comment, "Extremely mild ego drive, very unassertive. He'll avoid confrontation situations. If one occurs, he'll back down."

The ad director paused, and I agreed: "Right on."

There were more good things: Pays great attention to detail, social, creative.

Then came the verdict: "Lacks in a major way the inner need to persuade people. Absolutely not a salesperson. I'm very puzzled why he applied for a sales position." They recommended that I apply for a job in customer service.

I obtained a copy of the test results. The ad director would have hired me anyway; I had told him of my plans to use our Silva techniques to make some changes. But I decided I didn't want to sell advertising, I wanted to sell the Silva.

A little over two years later, I took a test administered to Silva lecturers by one of our researchers, Dr. George DeSau. We were looking for the personality traits of good lecturers, and this test measures sixteen personality factors.

The new test indicates that, in a group of peers, "potential for leadership is above average (the first time any test has given any hint of leadership ability for me), potential for success in jobs that reward interpersonal, sales, and persuasive skills is above average."

How to Change Personality

The test evaluates suitability for various occupations. My highest ratings were in areas of counseling, social work, business management, and high school teaching.

Grouped in with those was a "high" mark (7.7 on a scale with 10 as tops) as a real estate agent.

I had gained many new, desirable, personal characteristics without losing any of the good traits I had before.

What I Did To Make These Changes

What did I do to accomplish such a personality change in a little over two years?

Three broad steps were involved.

The first thing was awareness of my personality traits when I took the test. At the alpha level I was guided to seek help in sales. In the want ads of a daily newspaper was a very large advertisement seeking a "newspaper advertising sales representative." If I could sell anything, I reasoned, it should be newspaper advertising; I've been involved with the newspaper business my entire life.

The test I took when I applied for the job led me to realize, after studying some definitions in a dictionary, that I was very good at "convincing" people that the Silva is a fantastic program that could help them achieve great things, but I was no good at all in "persuading" people to take the training right now.

The second step was a lot of programming, using Silva techniques like Mirror of the Mind and 3-Fingers Technique.

The third step was objective: I took action.

The first thing I did was go to a flea market . . . and bargain for items! I used my 3-Fingers Technique to remind myself I had a persuasive personality, and it worked.

It has continued to work. And, according to the Cattell 16 Personality Factor test, it is an inner change that has taken place.

The bottom line, of course, relates to effectiveness. That is satisfactory: I now persuade more people to learn the Silva courses, and attendance at my lectures and my income have both increased. And most importantly to me: more people are now benefiting from the Silva techniques.

Yes, you can definitely develop the kind of personality you desire. If I can develop a persuasive, salesman's personality, then I am sure you can develop whatever personality you desire.

Go through the same three steps:

- Awareness of where you are and what is needed to get where you want to be (our many Silva techniques involving creative and intuitive thinking are excellent for this).
- Re-programming the bio-computer brain for the new personality.
- Take action in the physical world to support the programming.

Note: To learn more about the techniques mentioned in this chapter please see Resources (page 105).

Chapter 19

What Are Some Ways I Can Use The Silva ESP Techniques To Build Better Relationships?

by Silva Staff

At the end of every day, go to your center (the alpha level) and review the day.

Anything that did not go the way you want it to, correct it with the 3-Scenes Technique:

1. If there was something that you didn't like, visualize it in the first scene the way it happened. Then erase it and go to the second scene, towards your left.
2. In the second scene, change it so that the event unfolded in a different—better—way.
3. In the third scene, still further to your left, imagine a successful conclusion, where everybody benefits and all parties are satisfied and happy.

Can I Change Things That Other People Did?

You can use this technique for both yourself and for other people.

If you said something you wish you had not said, or did something you wish you had not done, then visualize it, erase it, and change it.

If you didn't say something that you wish now that you had said, or if you failed to do something that you wish you had done, use the 3-Scenes Technique to correct it.

If someone else said something that hurt you, or did something, or failed to say something or do something, then replay the event in the first scene, and correct it in the second scene.

Always finish with the third scene showing everybody happy with an outcome that was the best for everyone concerned.

What Does This Do To Change Things?

It won't change what happened. But by doing this, you can change the effect it had by neutralizing the negative energy that you have within yourself. When you do that, it will be easier for you to relate to the person the next time you see them.

If you missed an opportunity to tell somebody that you appreciate them, or something that they did, then go back and tell them, in the second scene. And program yourself to express your appreciation and your respect whenever the opportunity presents itself.

If someone failed to thank you or tell you that they appreciated something that you said or did, then go back and, in the white framed mirror, imagine them expressing their appreciation and respect. Then take it for granted that it happened; you'll feel better.

Besides your feeling better, as a graduate of José Silva's UltraMind ESP System, you know that when you are at your center, the alpha level, then you are able to project your mind anywhere that is necessary, to correct problems and improve conditions. So if you sincerely desire to make things better for everyone concerned, they will get the message.

Chapter 20

How Can I Attract Someone Into My Business or Personal Life?

by Ed Bernd Jr.

Use the MentalVideo Technique that José Silva gave us before his passing, advising us to allow room for higher intelligence to pair us up with the right person.

Avoid being too specific, he said. You may think you know what kind of person would be perfect for you, but remember that you don't know everything. Leave some room for higher intelligence to help you.

Here's an example:

There was a woman who wanted to find a man, and a man who wanted to find a woman. The man had heard that women often tend to marry a man because of the potential that they see in him, rather than for what he is right now.

He didn't want this kind of pressure, so he programmed to find a woman who would be happy with him the way he was.

Meanwhile the woman, who had heard that men tend to resist change, programmed to find a man who would be willing to change, to grow and to improve himself.

They got together, but they had a problem.

As the man began to move ahead in his career, his interests changed. His social activity changed, and his leisure time pursuits changed.

The woman didn't like this, because the things he was doing were different than what he did when they were courting. These were not the characteristics she had fallen in love with. When they had met, he was at a certain social level. She enjoyed his friends. Now he was making new friends, at a different level, and she was not comfortable with that.

Of course the man was dissatisfied also. He wanted his wife to grow along with him, but she resisted change. She wanted him to remain the way he was, which seemed very limiting to him.

They both got what they asked for, but neither of them got what they needed.

So What Is The Best Way To Program?

Be sure to leave some room for higher intelligence to find the person who is perfect for you. You can do it like this:

In your first MentalVideo, the one you create at the beta brain wave level, visualize yourself in your present situation. Then in the second MentalVideo, the one you create while at your level, imagine yourself in the situation you desire. Imagine yourself doing the kind of things you would like to be doing in this kind of relationship.

Do not be so specific that you rule out good possibilities. Leave room for your tutor on the other side to put you together with the best person for you.

Imagine the characteristics that you want the person to have, the most important characteristics. Do not rule out the perfect person because they have a different color hair, for instance.

Do not eliminate someone because they like different activities than you like, because you may find that there are things that you never experienced before, that you enjoy once you learn about them.

In your MentalVideo, imagine being with someone and the two of you being very happy that you are so compatible, that you have built such a good life for yourselves. Higher intelligence can then work out the details of how to bring this about.

During the day, look for indications . . . that is, keep an eye out for a person who might fit the bill, who might be the one that higher intelligence is sending to you.

Remember, too, that you might not meet Mr. Right or Ms. Right immediately. You might meet somebody else who can teach you something that you will need to know when the perfect person comes along.

What Would You Suggest I Do If I Am Having Problems In A Relationship, And I Don't Know Why?

First, think about it at your center. The alpha level is the ideal level for thinking.

Also pay attention to your dreams. Dreams are like postcards from the subconscious. Once you learn to interpret your dreams, they can give you a lot of information about yourself and your relationships.

One woman had a dream that she was a warrior, and realized that she was being too passive in her relationship with her boyfriend. She started making suggestions about where they could go on dates. It turned out that he liked this a lot. It was less pressure on him, and he felt more confident that they were doing something that she liked instead of her just going along with him to please him.

Chapter 21

(This is transcribed from a tape recording of Mr. Silva during an instructor training session in 1969)

How Can ESP Help Me Solve Problems?

by José Silva

Problem solving: It seems as though this is the only thing that we are on this planet for, to solve problems, and nothing else. All kinds of problems.

They say that problem solving makes for success.

How successful you are is how many problems you've solved.

Everything is problem solving.

And now because of this knowledge, that human intelligence can read, or sense, detect, information on other brains, wherever they are, the accumulation of knowledge, enhancement of wisdom, sensing other people's experiences, makes you a superior problem solving agent.

All kinds of problems.

Now of course the easiest information detected on any neurons, or brain cells, is information that has been impressed very strongly. If we have a weak impression, that will be more difficult to detect. We need to be more proficient in detecting on neurons, or brain cells.

The stronger the impression on brain cells, the easier it is to detect that information.

Distance is no barrier.

The kind of problem involved is a barrier, depending on how strong the impression is of such a problem. And usually the information that's strongly impressed on brain cells is information about stronger problems, and stronger means: The more value in the problem. The more serious the nature of the problem, the stronger the impression.

The more enthusiastic the person is about anything, the stronger the impression.

So an emotional involvement, we are saying: That is a factor. It will be a measure of how strong the impression. The more emotional the person, the stronger the impression.

People become emotional about problems. People become emotional about great things. So everything that's of importance, you can rest . . .

and be assured . . . it has been impressed very strongly because of its emotional involvement.

Minor things—things of very little value—are very faintly impressed, making it more difficult to detect this information. So the information that we use to detect it we say, is information of value, that has been strongly impressed because of emotional involvement. This is important of course for problem solving.

This is the information we need to solve problems with. Information that is necessary, that is valuable. Either because it was impressed for the survival type of response, the fight or flight type of response, which is strong emotional, or the enthusiastic type of discovery type of response that makes for development of problems.

So problem solving . . . tremendous.

Chapter 22

Can The UltraMind ESP System Help Me Pass A Test? I am a police officer and am preparing to take my captain's exam, which is necessary for me to get a promotion. Is it okay to use ESP to help me get the right answers?

by Ed Bernd Jr.

It is not cheating to use your mind to obtain the information you need to pass a test or solve a problem.

Any time you are doing any mental work, remember that the ideal brain wave level is the alpha level—your center.

When you function from the center of the brain frequency spectrum, you have access to information stored at the high beta (wide awake) frequencies, as well as the low theta frequencies that are typically associated with sleep and the so-called subconscious.

Once you have access to information impressed at the alpha and theta frequencies, it is no longer subconscious, or beneath conscious awareness. José Silva coined the term "inner conscious level" for this.

So your first step is to establish a good deep level of mind and learn to activate your mind and function at your center—the alpha level—with conscious awareness. The best tool for that is the Silva Centering Exercise which you can learn for free at the Silva7.com website.

Next, we suggest that you work on your motivation. José Silva always told us that when we are fulfilling our mission in life—which is to improve conditions on planet earth and make it a better place to live—then we will receive help from higher intelligence. The bigger your plans are, he said—meaning: the more people who will benefit—the more help you will receive.

If you do the motivation first, if you align yourself with higher intelligence and you believe that you are doing what God sent you here to do, and if you recall all of the benefits to yourself, your family, your friends, younger officers, and the people in the community—if you have all of that motivation and desire going for you, then your concentration will be great, your retention will be great, the adrenaline will be flowing, all of the information you have ever accumulated will be right there ready for you to use, and for anything you are not quite sure of, your intuition—your ESP—will be working at 100 percent!

If you are just doing it for yourself, and you don't care about anybody else, then you won't have all that focus and concentration and energy and drive.

You can start with the personal benefits, the self-interest. Then expand it out beyond, even beyond your own family, to the community.

Then go even farther, to your mission in life, and how your efforts, and how the even greater contributions you will make as a Captain, how this will be your way of fulfilling your mission in life, of doing what you were sent here to do.

This is your way of improving conditions on the planet, making the world a better place for all of the people that you protect and keep safe from evil, from the evil doers.

Couple all that with the ESP when you are taking the test and you are sure to pass.

Use ESP When Taking The Test

First of all, in order to help you retrieve the information that you have impressed on your brain cells, go to your center—the alpha level—and seek the information. It will be easier to detect from your center.

When you get to a question that you are not sure of, turn your eyes slightly upwards, defocus your vision (daydream), use your 3-Fingers Technique to trigger your intuition, and ask your Chief for the answer, or whoever is appropriate to ask.

Most police officers have great intuition or else they don't stay in the business very long. Recall the feeling you have when you see a car and "know" it should be stopped, and when you stop it, you find drugs or stolen property, etc. That's the feeling you want, when your ESP is working. Every police officer knows that feeling. You can't talk about it or the defense lawyers will eat you alive, but police officers know the feeling.

The written part of your examination is easy: You can turn your eyes upwards and defocus, and seek the answer.

When taking the verbal part of your examination, just do whatever you can. You can always get that "far away look" in your eyes, glance up, the way people do naturally when seeking an answer, and while glancing up, bring your three fingers together, relax, recall the feeling of being accurate on caseworking and in the field when you are on patrol, and say whatever comes to you.

The Bible says not to worry about what you are going to say; if your motives are right, then the right words will come to you.

Once you get the hang of it, you won't need any technique at all. You will recognize the feeling, and be aware of it when it comes, and be aware of what you do to trigger that feeling and to react to it, and what your attitude is, your emotions, etc. Then it will be a natural thing for you to do any time you need to use your ESP to get an answer and to know what to do.

There are specific speed learning and test taking techniques in the *Silva Choose Success Master Course*, featuring the original, authentic, unchanged techniques that José Silva developed during twenty-two years of scientific research.

There is information about it in the Resources (page 105).

Chapter 23

Guidelines For Getting Maximum Benefit From The Silva Techniques

1. Establish your level.

You must establish a deep level of mind. Everything works from that deep level of mind.

Here is how Juan Silva advises us to practice and establish a deep level as a baseline:

Learn the Long Relaxation Exercise (also called the Silva Centering Exercise)—the one where you "concentrate your sense of awareness on your scalp" and then "release and relax all tensions and ligament pressures . . ."

Memorize it—that is, learn the procedure and follow it. After you learn it you should not use a recording, and should not have anybody read it to you.

We do not want you to just learn all the words and repeat them by rote; that would not do you any good. The important thing is to learn what to do, step by step, and then do it.

Imagine that you can detect "a fine vibration, a tingling sensation, a feeling of warmth caused by circulation." Eventually you will actually begin to detect it. We don't instruct you to "feel" it—we want you to detect it with your mind. Remember what it feels like when you get a tingling sensation.

When you relax your scalp (and other parts of your body), how do you do that? How do you sense your scalp relaxing? Is it like a damp cloth over your skull? Are the roots of your hairs being washed with the warm blood circulation? How do you detect this relaxation?

It is important that you do it on your own, because nobody else knows what it takes for you to relax, how long it takes, what other parts of your body you need to relax. Nobody else knows how much you are hurting. Take as long as you need, to learn to totally relax your body, then your mind.

We recommend that new students practice the Long Relaxation Exercise at least once a week for the first three months. Many of us continue to practice it at least once a week, even twenty years later.

If you do not establish a good, deep level, then it will be difficult to get everything else to work for you. Once you establish that deep level, then everything else will begin to work for you.

2. Correct Sense Of Values

José Silva believed that we were sent here to correct problems, our own problems and problems of other people as well. He often said that the best way to help yourself is to find somebody else with the same problem and help them. People have long said that when we start teaching others is when we start to learn the most about the subject we are teaching.

Get together with other Silva graduates and program for their projects, and have them program for yours. Even if you don't know whether you are doing it correctly or not, do it anyway. This will help you learn to do it correctly.

If you don't know any other Silva graduates, tell your friends about the benefits and encourage them to take the course. They can learn in a live seminar, one of our home study courses, or some of our newest books. You can learn more about them in the Resources (page 105).

Keep one thing in mind: You should not offer to help them just because they are helping you; you should have a desire in yourself to help anyone who needs help, if you have an opportunity to help them.

Mr. Silva says that if we want help from higher intelligence, then we should be doing what we were sent here to do: Correcting problems.

The more problems you are solving, the more people you are helping, the more you qualify for help from higher intelligence.

If you are just working for yourself, and doing things for yourself only, then you are less likely to get help from higher intelligence. You are on your own. The techniques will still work for you, but it is much easier when you have help from other graduates, and from higher intelligence.

3. The Value Of Working Health Cases

Your intuition is to be used to help correct problems. It takes little time to work health detection and correction cases, and cost nothing.

When you work health cases, you could be helping people who don't even know you, who don't know that you are working in their behalf. This is a very unselfish act. And, as we mentioned above, when you are doing what you were sent here to do, you will prosper.

When Mr. Silva first started teaching the Silva course publicly, he had one student who could not work cases accurately. This student asked Mr. Silva what he should do. Mr. Silva told him to work 100 cases.

The student went to the person who had told him about the course—a nurse—and they met every afternoon after she got off work at the hospital, and she presented cases to him.

After he had worked 100 cases, he called Mr. Silva again and said that he still had not gotten any of them right, what should he do next?

Mr. Silva told him to work another 100 cases.

He did, still without success. So Mr. Silva told him to work another 100 cases.

Finally, about halfway through the third series of 100 cases, he began to get them right.

It paid off: He became one of our best psychics, was invited to join the headquarters staff, and became a vice president of the company and one of the best Silva instructors.

If you have enough desire, and if you persist, you will learn to do it, with or without your instructor's help. You can find graduates who are successful at working cases and get them to help you. Successful graduates love to solve problems, and will be happy to help you.

4. Improving Your Mental Skills

Whenever you get a technique to work for you, reinforce it: Enter your level and recall everything that you did. Use that success as a point of reference to help you have even more successes.

Every time you review a success at your level, it provides almost as much benefit as if you had actually had another success. Eventually, you will have accumulated enough energy from these successes (and remembered successes) that you can unlock another technique, and get it working for you.

Then the successes that you have with the two techniques will provide enough energy get yet another technique working for you.

You might not ever succeed with the third technique if you do not have successes with the first two. So keep trying different techniques until you find one that you can succeed at, so that you can build up that "success energy."

5. How To Make Sure Your Programming Is Working

Use feedback to help you:

- Whenever something works, and you get positive results, do more of it.

- If you try something several times and it doesn't work for you, then try something different.
- If you program for something and the situation gets worse, then enter your level, analyze the situation, and do the opposite of what you did before. If you start programming for a longer period of time and things get worse, then do the opposite: program for a shorter period of time and see what happens.

The point is, program for something where you can see results in a very short time, three or four days at the most. Then, whatever happens will guide you as to how to proceed: Whether to keep doing what you are doing, or to make adjustment.

That's one of the big advantages of working health cases as we do in the final part of the course: You get immediate feedback on every case that you work, so that you will know exactly how you are doing.

Once you start having success at detecting some of the problems you start comparing and contrasting your hits with your misses and figure out what to do to avoid misses and have more hits.

6. Advanced Programming Techniques

Use the formula-type techniques exactly as written. José Silva invested twenty-two years of scientific research to work out the exact wording and all of the details.

If you have a question about a technique, study the formula in your course manual; you will usually find the answer. Don't do what other people tell you to do if it conflicts with the formula. Do it José Silva's way.

For instance, some people used to think that they need to repeat their programming every day, or every three days. That's not what the formulas say: They say that "whenever you think of your project, visualize (recall) the solution image you created previously." Period. Follow the formulas exactly when you are learning.

Another tip is not to program for what you want. This is a problem-solving course, so program to solve a problem.

Instead of programming to get a lot of money, program to help people, and to keep your bills paid. Plan how you want to do it, and also leave some room for higher intelligence to contribute ideas that will work out the best for everybody concerned.

Remove all doubt about your programming. Use the alpha level to analyze problems and make decisions. You can also use Dream Control, or the MentalVideo when you get stuck, to help you program for the right thing.

Keep your programming in the possibility area. This does not mean to limit yourself, but if you program for something that you don't believe, deep inside, that you can achieve, there is little chance that you will achieve it, at least not any time soon.

Remember that we do not control other people. If somebody wants to drink and get drunk, they are going to drink and get drunk.

If a person wants to be with somebody else, it is a waste of time to program for that person to be with you.

You can program that a person will have a desire to change—to stop drinking, for instance. Once the person desires it enough, they will take the necessary steps to bring it about.

7. Visualization And Imagination

Visualization is recalling what something looks like that you have experienced before.

Imagination is thinking of what something looks like that you have never seen or imagined before.

For instance: Think of a dog that you have seen. Do you remember Lassie, from the television program and movies? Do you recall what the dog looked like? How many legs did the dog have? Four? When you do this, you are visualizing. You may have a vivid mental picture, or you may simply be recalling what the dog looked like—it is all visualization.

Now, imagine what that dog would look like if it had six legs. Where would the extra two legs go: in the front, the middle, the back? Imagine how funny that would look. When you do this, you are imagining.

Later, if you think about the dog with six legs, and recall what it would look like, then you are visualizing what you created with your imagination previously.

8. Suggested Practice Routines

Establish your level by practicing the Silva Centering (Long Relaxation) Exercise at least once a week.

Help fulfill your obligation by working health cases regularly. As a side benefit, you talents and abilities will improve.

Get your own life under control before you try to change the world. Some people want a job heading up a big company, yet they cannot even control their own bad habits, they suffer from tension and migraine headaches, they can't get a good night's sleep.

The better off you are in your personal life, the more value you will be to your employer.

Remember, program to correct problems. When you are a good enough problem solver, you will be rewarded handsomely for all of the problems you solve.

Remember that the most important time to practice is when you don't need to.

If you wait until you have a major problem, then the tension and worry will make it difficult for you to get to level and program correctly.

Practice when there's no pressure. Practice solving problems for members of your Silva Graduate Support Group. Help anyone who needs help.

Remember that if you only program for yourself, nobody else is going to be very interested in programming for you. The more help you give, the more help you will get when you need it. It may not come from the same people that you helped, but it will come.

9. Final Thoughts

If you review these guidelines from time to time and follow them, you will succeed.

Repeat the courses from time to time, and you will learn new things each time.

Work with other Silva graduates. Offer to help them in any way you can, and let them help you.

If you persist, you will succeed.

Resources

More books by these authors

Creative Coincidences
The Next Phase of Human Evolution
Influence the Coincidences in Your Life

Jose Silva's Everyday ESP Master Course
Unlock Your Natural God-Given Intuition a Complete Step-by-Step Guide

Jose Silva's Choose Success Master Course
Unleash Your Genius Mind Original Edition

For more books and to follow these authors:
amazon.com/author/josesilva
amazon.com/author/edberndjr

More Resources

Visit our website for our extensive knowledgebase, authentic José Silva courses, Silva Instructors and classes, and more: SilvaMethodUltraMind.com

www.ingramcontent.com/pod-product-compliance
Lightning Source LLC
Chambersburg PA
CBHW061745050726
47598CB00002B/599
* 9 7 8 1 7 2 2 5 0 7 6 7 1 *